# Wild Britain

# Blackbird

Louise and Richard Spilsbury

www.heinemann.co.uk
Visit our website to find out more information about **Heinemann Library** books.

To order:
☎ Phone 44 (0) 1865 888066
▤ Send a fax to 44 (0) 1865 314091
▢ Visit the Heinemann Bookshop at www.heinemann.co.uk to browse our catalogue and order online.

First published in Great Britain by Heinemann Library, Halley Court, Jordan Hill, Oxford OX2 8EJ, part of Harcourt Education Ltd. Heinemann is a registered trademark of Harcourt Education Ltd.

Editorial: Lucy Thunder and Helen Cox
Design: David Poole and Celia Floyd
Illustrations: Jeff Edwards, Alan Fraser and Geoff Ward
Picture Research: Catherine Bevan and Maria Joannou
Production: Séverine Ribierre

Originated by Dot Gradations
Printed and bound in Hong Kong, China by South China Printing

ISBN 0 431 03932 1 (hardback)
07 06 05 04 03
10 9 8 7 6 5 4 3 2 1

ISBN 0 431 03939 9 (paperback)
07 06 05 04 03
10 9 8 7 6 5 4 3 2 1

**British Library Cataloguing in Publication Data**
Spilsbury, Louise and Spilsbury, Richard
Blackbird. – (Wild Britain)
598.8'74
A full catalogue record for this book is available from the British Library.

**Acknowledgements**

The Publishers would like to thank the following for permission to reproduce photographs:

Corbis p14 (Roger Wilmshurst), 15 (Eric & David Hosking); FLPA pp5 (Neil Bowman), 9, 16, 28 (Roger Wilmshurst), 11 (David Hosking), 13, 20 (Eric & David Hosking), 21 (Peggy Heard), 24 (Minden Pictures), 25 (D T Grewcock); Nature Photographers pp22 (Colin Carver), 29 (E A Janes); NHPA p6 (Laurie Campbell); OSF p18 (Richard Packwood); Oxford Scientific Films p4 (Tony Tilford); Papilio p27 (Phillip Marazzi); Premaphotos Wildlife p12 (Ron Brown); Robert Pickett p7; RSPCA Photo Library pp8 (Mark Hamblin), p10 (E A Janes); p23 (Colin Varndell); Sylvia Cordaiy Pic Library p19; Windrush Photos p26 (G Langsbury).

Cover photograph of a male blackbird, reproduced with permission of the National Photographic Library (Niall Benvine, Nature Picture Library).

The Publishers would like to thank Michael Scott for his assistance in the preparation of this book.

Every effort has been made to contact copyright holders of any material reproduced in this book. Any omissions will be rectified in subsequent printings if notice is given to the Publishers.

# Contents

Any words appearing in the text in bold, **like this**, are explained in the Glossary.

# What are blackbirds?

Adult male blackbirds, like this, are usually about 25 centimetres long.

Blackbirds are one of the most common birds in Britain. **Male** blackbirds are easy to recognize. They are black with a yellow **beak** and a yellow ring around their eyes.

This is a female blackbird. Her yellow beak is easy to spot. It is paler than the male's beak.

**Female** blackbirds are dark brown. A female's yellow beak is not as bright as a male's. Females usually have a speckled belly and a pale chin.

# Where blackbirds live

Many blackbirds live in gardens and parks.

Blackbirds live where there are trees and bushes for them to hide in. You often see blackbirds looking for food in short grass or piles of leaves under bushes and trees.

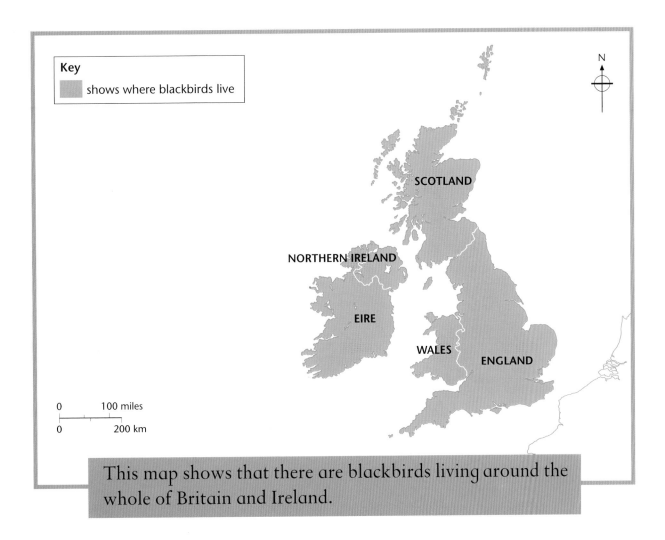

N

SCOTLAND

NORTHERN IRELAND

EIRE

WALES

ENGLAND

0     100 miles

0          200 km

This map shows that there are blackbirds living around the whole of Britain and Ireland.

Blackbirds live almost everywhere in Britain, except high hills and mountains. They live in woodlands, farmland, marshes, parks, gardens and by sandy coasts.

# What blackbirds eat

In spring, there are lots of earthworms around that blackbirds can catch easily.

Blackbirds eat lots of different kinds of food. In spring and summer, they usually eat earthworms, slugs and **insects** such as small beetles.

Holly and ivy berries are good for blackbirds to eat late in winter, when there is little other food about.

In autumn and winter, blackbirds mostly eat berries from plants. Blackbirds also need water. They drink water from puddles or garden birdbaths.

# Finding food

This blackbird is listening out for worms that come near the surface of the **soil**.

Blackbirds spend a lot of time on the ground searching for food. They hop around, listening carefully for worms and **insects** moving under the grass.

A blackbird's beak is sharp and pointy for spearing food. It is also thick and strong for crushing food.

When a blackbird finds a worm or an insect in the ground, it tugs out the food with its sharp, strong **beak**.

# On the move

When a blackbird is on the ground, its **wings** are folded into its body.

Blackbirds run or hop along the ground with their long tail up. They stop often to check for danger. They run under a bush or fly up to a tree if something frightens them.

When blackbirds fly, they open their wings wide. They flap them to move through the air.

Like other birds, blackbirds fly by opening and flapping their wings. They use their tail **feathers** as brakes to slow themselves down.

13

# Resting and sleeping

Blackbirds sleep at night. They rest in trees so they can hide from animals that try to eat them.

Blackbirds rest and sleep on branches in trees or bushes. The leaves **protect** them from bad weather and keep them hidden from **predators**.

This blackbird is flying off to find food. It will return to the same tree to rest at night.

On cold winter nights, blackbirds sleep together in groups called **roosts**. It is warmer to sleep in a roost and there are more birds to warn if a predator comes near.

# A blackbird's nest

This blackbird is collecting materials to build a nest.

Blackbirds do not live in nests. They make nests when they are ready to **lay** their eggs. They build a nest in a tree, hedge, rooftop or sometimes on the ground.

Female blackbirds usually lay four or five eggs at a time.
The eggs are a blue-green colour with reddish spots.

**Female** blackbirds usually make the nest.
They stick twigs, leaves and moss together
with mud and spit. They put grass or dead
leaves inside to make a soft bed for the eggs.

# Blackbird young

Baby blackbirds kick and peck their way out of their eggs using their legs and **beaks**.

The **female** blackbird sits on the eggs to keep them warm. This helps the baby birds inside to grow. After about two weeks the baby birds **hatch** out of the eggs.

These blackbird chicks are only two days old.

Young blackbirds are called **chicks**. For the first eight days their eyes are closed. They have few **feathers** and they are helpless. Their parents feed them and look after them.

# Growing up

Blackbird chicks call out to tell their parents they are hungry. Parent birds drop worms into their open mouths.

**Chicks** spend the first two weeks of their life in the nest. Their parents bring them earthworms to eat. Chicks get all the water they need from the food they eat.

Young blackbirds are light brown with pale spots. They get their darker adult **feathers** at about six months old.

After two weeks, young blackbirds leave the nest. They learn to fly and find food by watching their parents. At six weeks old they fly away to live by themselves.

# Blackbird sounds

Male blackbirds usually sing from a high perch, like a high branch or chimney.

**Male** blackbirds sing in spring and summer to attract a **female** to have young with. Some people say they sound like a flute playing.

When blackbirds meet in roosts they make loud 'dik-dik' sounds to each other.

Blackbirds living in towns and cities face many dangers. They make a loud chattering noise to warn other blackbirds of danger.

# Under attack

Sparrowhawks, like this one, are fast and strong.

Magpies, crows and grey squirrels sometimes eat blackbird eggs or **chicks**. Sparrowhawks are large **birds of prey** that eat adult blackbirds.

One way to help garden birds is to put a bell on your cat's collar so birds can hear it coming.

Pet cats are a danger to blackbirds living in gardens and parks. People who study blackbirds think that pet cats kill more blackbirds than any other **predator**.

# Dangers

Cars may run over blackbirds feeding at the roadside.

Many blackbirds live in towns and cities.
There are problems with living in town,
though. Sometimes, blackbirds are killed
by traffic on the roads.

This garden hedge has been cut at the wrong time of year. Predators can easily see the chicks inside this blackbird nest.

Many blackbirds make nests in hedgerows. If people cut hedges in spring and early summer, **predators** can easily find the eggs and **chicks** in their nests.

# A blackbird's year

Blackbirds lay their first clutch (set) of eggs early in spring.

Blackbirds may **lay** a set of eggs two or three times a year. Most blackbird babies are born in spring. It is warmer then and there are lots of earthworms to eat.

When it is very cold in winter, you can help by putting out extra food, like apples, for blackbirds.

In autumn, blackbirds **moult**. Their old **feathers** drop out. They grow new ones ready for winter. In winter, when it is very cold, it is hard for blackbirds to find food.

# Animal groups

Scientists group together birds that are alike. Blackbirds belong to the thrush group. Other thrushes include the song thrush and redwing.

blackbird

redwing

song thrush

The artwork on this page is not to scale.

# Glossary

**beak** hard, pointed part of a bird's mouth

**birds of prey** large, strong birds that hunt and catch other animals for food

**chick** young bird that is not yet fully grown

**feathers** soft covering which keeps a bird warm and helps it to fly

**female** animal which can become a mother when it is grown up. A female human is called a woman or a girl.

**hatch** to be born from an egg

**insect** small animal that has six legs when an adult

**lay** when an egg comes out from a female animal's body

**male** animal which can become a father when it is grown up. A male human is called a man or a boy.

**moult** when an animal loses its feathers or fur and grows a new set

**predator** animal that catches and eats other animals for food

**protect** keep something safe from harm

**roost** place where lots of birds rest or sleep together

**scientist** person who studies the world around us and the things in it to find out how they work

**soil** also called earth. Soil is made up of tiny bits of rock and dead plants and animals.

**wings** birds have a wing on each side of their body. They use them to fly.

# Index

# Titles in the *Wild Britain* series include:

Hardback          0 431 03928 3

Hardback          0 431 03932 1

Hardback          0 431 03930 5

Hardback          0 431 03931 3

Hardback          0 431 03933 X

Hardback          0 431 03929 1

Find out about the other titles in this series on our website www.heinemann.co.uk/library